# Clean and Friendly
# for More Than
# 25 Years

# Clean and Friendly for More Than 25 Years

## The Super 8 Story

*Jack El-Hai*

Greenwich Publishing Group, Inc., Lyme, Connecticut

Produced and published by
Greenwich Publishing Group, Inc., Lyme, Connecticut

Design by Elaine Rentz Design

Separation and film assembly by Scan Communications Group, Inc.

All photographs and artifacts courtesy of Super 8 Motels, Inc.
Photography of Super 8 Motels artifacts by Christopher Devlin Brown.

The following are registered service marks of TM Acquisition Corp., an
affiliate of Super 8 Motels, Inc.:
     America's Finest Economy Lodging
     Super 8
     Superline
     We're Pineapple Kind of People
     Super 8 Motel Logo

The following are service marks of TM Acquisition Corp., an affiliate of
Cendant Corporation:
     Days Inn
     Howard Johnson
     Knights Inn
     Travelodge
     Villager Lodge
     Wingate Inn

The Ramada service mark is utilized by Ramada Franchise Systems,
Inc., under license from Franchise Systems Holdings, Inc.

Library of Congress Card Number: 99-66736

ISBN: 0-944641-37-7

First Printing: September 1999

10 9 8 7 6 5 4 3 2 1

**American Express is proud to make this commemorative book available to you!**

**Cards**

As many of you know, American Express has been a dedicated partner of Super 8 Motels for many years — and is committed to Super 8's continued success. Whether through marketing programs or sponsorship of annual Super 8 conferences, American Express is proud to contribute to the long-term strength and professional development of this franchise and the lodging industry as a whole.

We also recognize the tremendous achievements of Super 8, both on behalf of its valued employees and for its customers. Recently, American Express, together with the American Hotel & Motel Association, sponsored a study by Cornell University to examine best practices in the lodging industry. Entitled *American Lodging Excellence*, the study examined more than 3,500 individual nominations before the researchers selected 144 "best practice champions." Among those recognized for outstanding achievement was Super 8. The study noted that "because of the focus on hospitality, Super 8 has developed an enviable consistency in the definition of the product and service."

American Express is also committed to excellence and to providing our merchant partners and Cardmembers with outstanding services and benefits. Whether guests are traveling close to home or abroad, they can always count on the American Express® Card to help make traveling worry free. With CARDeposit, guests have a convenient way to protect their reservations at hotels that require an advance deposit. And they always have the convenience of 24-hour Customer Service wherever they go.

We look forward to working with you for many years to come and know you'll continue to benefit from the ongoing partnership between American Express and Super 8.

**Congratulations on 25 years of providing high-quality service in the lodging industry!**

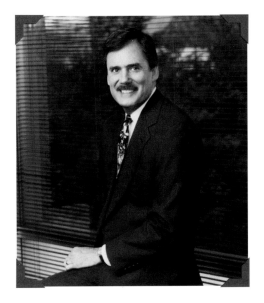

*T*he fall of 1999 marks the 25th anniversary celebration of one of the great success stories in U.S. lodging and franchising history — Super 8 Motels.

It would be a major achievement if Super 8 had only its dynamic growth to demonstrate its success. But here is a company that has offered so much more to its franchise owners, its employees and its guests. Super 8 is a company that, from day one, recognized and practiced the human side of enterprise.

No introduction to a Super 8 documentary would be proper without mention of the bold Dakotans who set the pace for the company. The leadership of Ron Rivett and Dennis Brown — and later Dennis Bale, Loren Steele and Harvey Jewett — was readily identified by their perseverance, their passion and, most importantly, their character. Their consistent management philosophies throughout the founding years enabled those who came later to maintain the company's great momentum.

There continues to be, after 25 years of operation, a real spirit within Super 8 as a company and a passion that drives its people. This anniversary story of Super 8 Motels is about that spirit and passion, and why we are able to say, "Life's great at Super 8!"

*Robert N. Weller, President*
*September 1999*

## TABLE OF CONTENTS

# A Great Idea

**B**uilt in 1974 without an architect's plan and managed by a teen fresh out of high school, the first Super 8 motel launched a fledgling lodging company on a remarkable path. Here in their home-town of Aberdeen, South Dakota, Super 8 founders Dennis Brown and Ron Rivett learned their first lessons in designing, furnishing, staffing and raising funds for a successful economy motel.

**A**t a coffee shop in Aberdeen, South Dakota, two acquaintances sometimes got together to discuss schemes and dreams. They were Dennis Brown, attorney and visionary, and Ron Rivett, an experienced financier of home and office construction. One day in 1973, Brown took a gulp of coffee and described to Rivett a business phenomenon he had noticed a few years earlier while working for the IRS in California. Budget-priced motels, he said, were springing up along the West Coast. Usually faced with a choice between Mom and Pop motels of unpredictable quality and expensive hotels, business travelers were responding well to the new availability of brand-name motels offering low rates.

**I**n a single day in 1973, Super 8 Motels went from an idea discussed over coffee to an incorporated business that would take the lodging industry by storm.

No one had brought this idea to the Midwest yet, and the two men talked about starting a chain of economy motels. "I knew the idea would work," Brown later said. "It was obvious that with inflation getting so out of hand, people sooner or later wouldn't be able to afford traveling any other way." And even when the economy improved, he believed, economy motels of high quality would continue to attract guests interested in clean rooms and low prices.

Rivett listened intently. He knew that financing motels wasn't easy, but something about Brown's ideas intrigued him. And lacking savings or assets, neither man had much to lose. The two kept talking, left the coffee shop, and found themselves standing together at a parking meter, unable to let the idea drop. "Finally I said to him, 'How about building a motel?'" Rivett says. He speculated that the best way to make an economy motel chain work would be to start fresh, building new motels that looked and felt as alike as McDonald's restaurants. Brown agreed and suggested they continue their conversation later that day.

When Brown again met Rivett that afternoon, he brought along a stock certificate he had drawn up for a new company, with each of the men owning 50 percent of the shares. From its humble beginnings in a coffee shop, the brainstorming of Brown and Rivett has since grown into one of the world's largest chains of economy motels — Super 8.

What these South Dakotans envisioned was a motel chain built around the philosophy of providing consistent, friendly service and clean rooms year-round at rates substantially lower than those of surrounding hotels and motels. Unlike some other economy chains of the day, the rooms would include such amenities as direct-dial phones and TV sets. Guests, primarily business travelers, would receive the basic features of a more expensive motel without the unnecessary extras that drove up the price. The encouraging successes of other early economy motel chains convinced them that their idea could fly.

It was more than a good business plan that gave Brown and Rivett cause for optimism. The two men were perfect complements to each other's talents. Brown was the creative thinker, the one with foresight and daring. The favorite game of his childhood was Monopoly, and as an adult, he still loved the entrepreneurial excitement of creating new businesses. Already he had started new businesses

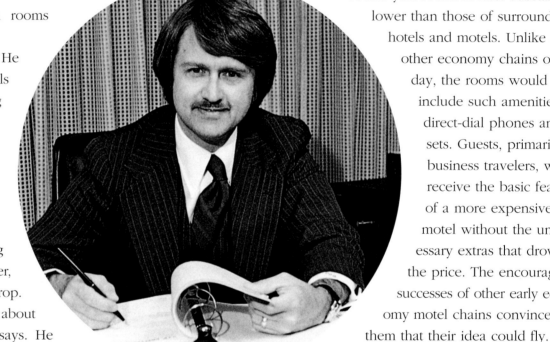

Co-founder Dennis Brown started several businesses before discovering in Super 8 a commercial venture that really took off. It was Brown who first recognized the nationwide potential of an economy motel chain and came up with the Super 8 name.

devoted to publishing legal books, marketing toys, selling tornado alarms, distributing wallet-sized microfiches of the owner's medical history and manufacturing pantyhose. In 1972, Brown attempted to organize a marketing association of existing economy motels in the upper Midwest under the name Super 8, but it generated no income.

Rivett had just resigned as a bank trust officer in order to sell insurance and real estate. He had the practical knowledge of financing and construction to oversee the planning and building of the actual motels. "We were poor," Rivett says, "but we worked very well together. We could go our separate way for 10 days and not talk to each other, and then come back and find we'd both been thinking in the same direction."

Brown dissolved his motel association and they decided to reuse Super 8 as the name of their new motel chain. "I chose the name Super 8 Motel because I wanted to charge around $8.00 a night, and 'super' is the first word to come to mind," Brown wrote in his unpublished memoirs. "Many people think all brand names come from extensive market research costing hundreds of thousands of dollars. Obviously mine didn't."

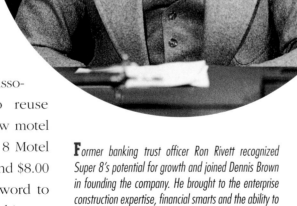

*F*ormer banking trust officer Ron Rivett recognized Super 8's potential for growth and joined Dennis Brown in founding the company. He brought to the enterprise construction expertise, financial smarts and the ability to set in motion the visionary dreams of his partner.

## Opening in Aberdeen

The partners were confident of their idea, but potential lenders weren't easily convinced that a new motel chain starting out in the Midwest would succeed. When local banks wouldn't lend the money for the purchase of land, Brown and Rivett asked a friend to help raise money from small investors. "We picked the best location in Aberdeen," Rivett notes — just down the road from a Holiday Inn. For the company's first several years, finding land near Holiday Inns remained the primary strategy for new locations.

Finding financing for the construction of the first motel took longer. But by the spring of 1974, the money was in hand. Rivett began designing the motel. "We didn't even have a real set of plans," he says. "I just drew it on a piece of paper without the proper engineering or architectural stamps. For the exterior, someone suggested using stucco, which was a great idea because my father-in-law was a stuccoer. We wanted a look that would stand out, so we did some cross-hatching on the outside." Thus was born the English Tudor look that represented Super 8 for many years.

In September 1974, the first Super 8 motel was open for business in Aberdeen. It had 60 rooms and little

## $8.88? That's Super!

Super 8 has a common sense approach to away-from-home lodging. When it comes right down to it, what do you really need when you're looking for a motel room? A clean, comfortable room with a good bed, TV, direct dial phone, combination tub & shower & quietness. Above all, a reasonable price. How does $8.88 single, $10.88 double suit you?

What does Super 8 eliminate? A bar, expensive lobby areas, a swimming pool. They're fine for some occasions, but not when all you really want is a good night's sleep.

Super 8 is now the 6th largest budget motel chain in the US. Its national average occupancy, over 80 percent, is due to the satisfaction of repeat customers. The Nov-issue of "Real Estate Appraiser" listed Super 8 as one of the fastest growing motel chains. It has motel-members in Maine, Minn, South Carolina & Utah.

Super 8 expands to Pierre, Mitchell & Yankton by early summer. Then Miller, Rapid City, North Sioux City. In Mpls & St Paul, 5 locations soon! And in Iowa: Cedar Rapids, West Des Moines & Adventureland.

Super 8 invites regular travelers to join its "Salesmen's Club." Get your card punched each time for 9-nites' lodging. Stay a 10th nite free.

Super 8 sez, "On your next trip, stay with us. You won't regret it, neither will your budget."

W&W sez, "It all started here in November '74. Super 8 may put Abdn on the nationwide map like nothing since the quints."

Franchises for new locations are available; writ Box 1456, Abdn, SD 57401.

Abdn's **Super 8 Motel** makes sense. The prototype for rapidly expanding Super 8 is the 60-unit budget motel on East Highway 12 at Roosevelt Road. Join their "Salesmen's Club"!

---

# 60-unit motel is planned

CONSTRUCTION is to begin by April 1 on a 60-unit Super 8 motel on 6th Ave. S.E. north of the former Ranch Cafe location.

Site preparation is presently under way there.

The Super 8 franchise is owned by Dennis Brown and Ronald J. Rivett and is headquartered in Aberdeen. Brown says 19 independently-owned motels throughout the country are part of the chain.

Brown said the motel here will be owned by individuals from the Aberdeen area.

Brown said manager of the new motel will be Milo Graff, who is now associated with the Breeze Inn Motel.

Brown said the motel will have only motel units and live-in quarters for the manager but, he added, all Super 8 motels are located within walking distance of a restaurant.

---

**J**ust six months after its founding, Super 8 already ranked as the nation's sixth-largest economy motel chain, according to this news clip, left. The $8.88 rate didn't last long, but it generated early media attention and return customers right from the start. The Super 8 Salesmen's Club, below, was an early promotion offering a 10th night of lodging free as a reward for this loyalty. As the 1974 clip at right shows, Brown and Rivett initially planned to link their first Super 8 in Aberdeen with other independently owned motels in the region. The partners soon discarded this plan in favor of franchising additional Super 8 motels.

---

landscaping. Barbara Brown, Dennis' wife, helped shop for room furnishings. "I remember selecting carpets and bedspreads and buying soap," she says. "Everything was blue and orange, including the shag carpets and the floral print bedspreads." The room rate was set at $8.88 a night, a low price but, nonetheless, one that established the fledgling chain as a cut above such bare-bones competitors as Motel 6, which offered rooms at $6.66.

Soon after the motel's opening, the fall pheasant hunting season began in South Dakota, getting the motel off to a good start with plenty of sportsmen guests. "We were doing well in October and November, but then it was slow in December, January and February," remembers Milo Graff, who became the chain's first motel manager straight out of high school, at the age of 18. "Occupancy was running about 50 percent and the motel was operating okay. Dennis and Ron were concerned, though, because they had projected we'd do better."

Just in time to avert financial trouble, help came from the most reassuring source possible — repeat business from satisfied customers. "All of a sudden, guests began coming back. Guys in the sales trade were returning, and we continued to make new clientele," Graff says. "When March of 1975 came, occupancy was right at 80 percent, and it took off from there."

Soon financing was in place for three other motels in the South Dakota towns of Pierre, Mitchell and Yankton. Brown saw his vision coming together. Milo Graff remembers the day Dennis told him, "I can see that someday we will have upwards of 150 motels in this chain." Graff held back a laugh and thought to himself growth of that scale would never happen.

Brown and Rivett knew the only way to build a chain of more than a handful of motels was to franchise the

**S**ix Super 8 motels already stood along the highways of three states when this brochure, right, promoted the Aberdeen member of the chain. The most financially savvy guests paid attention to a line on an inner page of the brochure: "Super 8 franchises are available." Milo Graff, at 20 years old the chain's veteran motel manager, receives thanks in 1977 from then-president Dennis Bale. Graff currently owns several Super 8 properties.

Super 8 name. It was a tricky step. They needed people willing to raise their own money and uphold the same high standards set by Brown and Rivett. The idea of franchising lodging businesses had been initiated years earlier by C. Kemmons Wilson, founder of Holiday Inn. Wilson had built a chain of consistently good roadside properties that guests could rely on. But because they attracted customers with restaurants and bars that lost money, they had to subsidize the food and beverage operations with a higher room rate. Brown

Super 8's first annual convention, left, held in Aberdeen in 1977, brought together 90 owners, managers, housekeepers and Super 8 staff. About 25 motels then formed the chain.

**1976, First newsletter** for franchisees, typed and photocopied on three sheets of paper, referring to all home office employees by their first names only

**1976, First wedding** held at a Super 8 motel in Mobridge, South Dakota, joining Saundra and Ray McKittrick

**1977, First convention** for franchisees in Aberdeen, South Dakota

**1974, First motel,** Aberdeen, South Dakota

**1974, First employee,** Ron Reed, hired as director of management and sole motel inspector

**1975, First franchised motel,** Gillette, Wyoming

**1975, First reservation** made on Super 8's national toll-free line, a reservation for the motel in Gillette, Wyoming

**1977, First V.I.P. Club member,** Nancy Hernandez, a vending machine sales person living in Fargo, North Dakota

Three people — Ron Reed, Dennis Brown, and JoAnn LaBay — were the core of Super 8's "HQ" during the mid-1970s. Reed was the company's first employee, and LaBay joined soon afterward as an administrative assistant.

In 1978, franchisee Shirley Davies won the first Super 8 Motel of the Year Award, — presented in 1979 by Dennis Bale (left) — an honor that later bore her name.

**1978, First Shirley Davies Award of Excellence** presented for the Motel of the Year

**1979, First computer** owned by Super 8, an IBM Office System 6, used for word processing, corporate record-keeping, and processing V.I.P. Club applications

**1981, First Canadian motel,** in North Battleford, Saskatchewan

**1983, First U.S. motel outside** the continental U.S., Ketchikan, Alaska

### HURON, SOUTH DAKOTA

We wanted to congratulate you on running the most courteous, clean and welcoming hotel we have ever stayed at. All of your staff treated us with true warmth and friendliness. Everyone we came in contact with was accommodating and willing to do anything to make our stay a more pleasant one. Thanks again for a wonderful experience, and we will see you next year. We enjoyed ourselves so much, we have decided to make pheasant hunting there an annual trip.

*Ed & Kathy H., Luzerne, Michigan*

and Rivett set out to find a franchise formula that would consistently combine quality lodging with low room rates.

Harvey Jewett spent four years as Super 8's outside attorney before joining the company as general counsel in 1978. He later served as Super 8's chief operating officer and president.

## The Franchise Formula

Brown and Rivett sold their first franchise in 1976 to a motel developer in Gillette, Wyoming. Other franchisees emerged in Dickinson, North Dakota; Brookings, South Dakota; and Sheridan, Wyoming. These initial franchise agreements were drawn up by a young attorney named Harvey Jewett. They gave each franchise owner a guaranteed geographic radius of

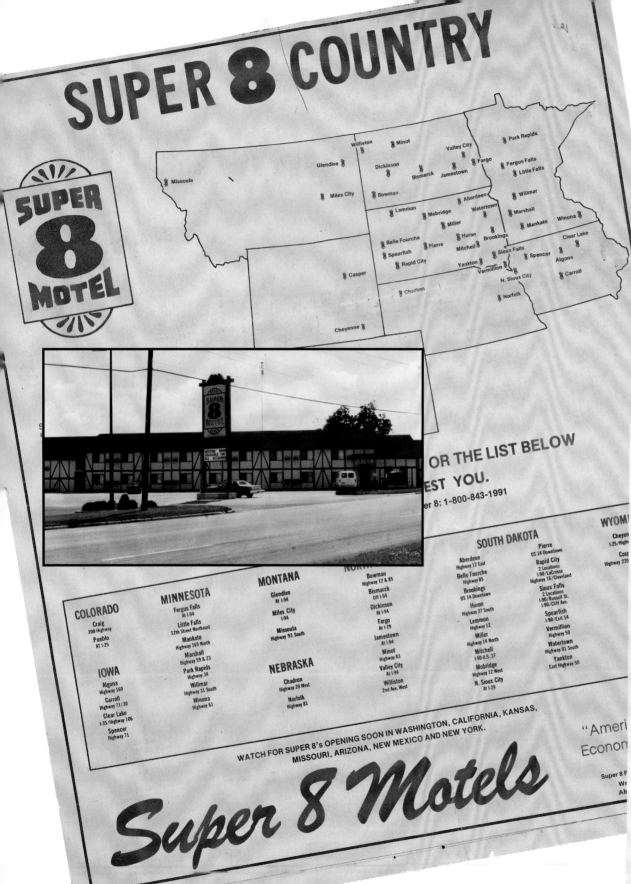

# SUPER 8 COUNTRY

**SUPER 8 MOTEL**

**Super 8 Motels**

... OR THE LIST BELOW
... EST YOU.
...er 8: 1-800-843-1991

### COLORADO
Craig
200 Highway
Pueblo
AT I-25

### IOWA
Algona
Highway 169
Carroll
Highway 71/30
Clear Lake
I-35/Highway 106
Spencer
Highway 71

### MINNESOTA
Fergus Falls
At I-94
Little Falls
12th Street Northeast
Mankato
Highway 169 North
Marshall
Highway 59 & 23
Park Rapids
Highway 34
Willmar
Highway 31 South
Winona
Highway 61

### MONTANA
Glendive
At I-94
Miles City
I-94
Missoula
Highway 93 South

### NEBRASKA
Chadron
Highway 20 West
Norfolk
Highway 81

### NORTH ...
Bowman
Highway 12 & 85
Bismarck
Off I-94
Dickinson
At I-94
Fargo
At I-29
Jamestown
At I-94
Minot
Highway 83
Valley City
At I-94
Williston
2nd Ave. West

### SOUTH DAKOTA
Aberdeen
Highway 12 East
Belle Fourche
Highway 85
Brookings
US 14 Downtown
Huron
Highway 37 South
Lemmon
Highway 12
Miller
Highway 14 North
Mitchell
I-90-U.S. 37
Mobridge
Highway 12 West
N. Sioux City

Pierre
US 14 Downtown
Rapid City
2 Locations
I-90/LaCrosse
Highway 16/Cleveland
Sioux Falls
2 Locations
I-90/Russell St.
I-90/Cliff Ave.
Spearfish
I-90/Exit 14
Vermillion
Highway 50
Watertown
Highway 81 South
Yankton
East Highway 50

### WYOMI...
Cheyen...
I-25/Highw...
Casp...
Highway 220...

WATCH FOR SUPER 8's OPENING SOON IN WASHINGTON, CALIFORNIA, KANSAS, MISSOURI, ARIZONA, NEW MEXICO AND NEW YORK.

"Ameri...
Econom...

Super 8 F...
Wr...
Ab...

**SUPER 8**

**What Is Super 8?**

**Opportunity!**

**And More . . .**

When Super 8 began courting franchisees in 1974, the franchise fee was $10,000. The brochure for prospective owners below encourages them to become part of "America's fastest-growing budget motel franchise." By the time this newspaper ad ran in 1978, left, the company's expansion had taken it into eight Midwestern states, with new locations springing up all the time. The inset shows the Super 8 motel in Creston, Iowa, which opened later that year on September 19. It was the first motel owned by Supertel Hospitality, Inc. In time, Supertel would grow into one of the company's largest franchisees.

protection and assistance in building, furnishing and marketing the new motels. In addition, Super 8 promised franchisees help in developing accounting and other business systems, as well as centralized reservation services. In return, the franchised Super 8 motels paid a monthly franchise fee to the company and had to submit to quarterly quality inspections.

Most of the new franchisees had no previous experience in the lodging business. "We were the partners of these people," says Jewett. "They had to succeed in order to pay their royalties. So we realized that in order for Super 8 to do well, we had to get along with the franchisees. They didn't have to buy a damn thing from us. But we did make every franchisee come to Aberdeen and see how our reservation center worked, how we did our training and how we offered franchise services. They would sit with the inspector and learn our standards. Then we'd take them to dinner, which wasn't always convenient, but it was important to establish a personal relationship with them."

Many of those dinners in the early days were served in the home of Loren Steele, a banker who joined the Super 8 management in 1977 as executive vice president. "You could say we were aggressive in entertaining prospects," he says. "In a social atmosphere, you

*U*pon becoming Super 8 president in 1976, Dennis Bale immediately began traveling the country to visit potential franchisees. He delivered his Super 8 pitch in bars, banks and even dirty old pickup trucks.

can determine a person's character."

Unlike some other franchised businesses, Super 8 preferred not to use psychological profiles to screen prospective franchisees. It was a decision made from the gut. And for the most part, those who made the grade contributed enormously to the chain's success.

## Not a "Slick" Operation

Super 8 had quickly become a business that required full-time attention, although both Brown and Rivett kept other businesses going for a few years. In 1975, Super 8 moved into its own offices at 224 6th Avenue Southeast in Aberdeen and set up a small staff. The first hire was Ron Reed, the director of management who personally performed all motel inspections. Dave Blackmun was later hired to head up Midwest Restaurant Supply Company, a Super 8 partner that supplied motels with furnishings, supplies, printed goods and equipment, and Keith Peterson headed another affiliated company that constructed motels.

During those early years, Super 8 was a quaint, even primitive operation. In 1976, the company's newsletter to franchisees reported that an office assistant had filed the Super 8 Christmas card list under "miscellaneous," but had also created a file called

"Christmas List" which contained only a note saying, "Look for Christmas card list under 'Miscellaneous.'" The newsletter concluded: "Only a person who has opened the files in this office can appreciate the logic of this."

But there was lots of important work to do. In 1976, Super 8 hired Dennis Bale, another banker, as Super 8's new president. His main job was to relieve Dennis Brown of the sole responsibility for cultivating prospective franchisees. "I was a little hesitant about joining the Super 8 team for a number of reasons," Bale admitted in a message to franchisees. "But after several visits with Dennis Brown and Ron Rivett, I began to realize the magnitude and potential of Super 8. The story not only intrigued me, but literally excited me."

Awaiting Bale on his first day at Super 8 was a seven-page, single-spaced memo from Brown explaining all of the company's plans and pending projects. Bale immediately got to work meeting with prospective franchisees. "Selling franchises was tricky," he remembers. "We had to make sure we were properly registered with each state and had satisfied their franchising laws. I remember once talking with a franchisee in the back seat of a dirty old Chevrolet next to the family dog. I talked with people from every background — from bartenders to bankers."

## Setting a Faster Pace

At first, the number of franchisees was small. "In the early days, 10 or 12 of them would sit around and discuss which detergents and carpet cleaners to use," says Dale Aasen, now the company's regional vice president of franchise sales. The days of such intimate meetings were numbered. Franchise requests began to come in at a fast pace. There were 22 Super 8 motels by the fall of 1976. "Last week must have set an all-time record high in

Initially hired in 1975 as an administrative assistant, JoAnn LaBay later moved up to Super 8's director of franchisee relations. Her signature appears on an early free-night stay promotional card, a guest perk available in certificate form today.

Aberdeen American News Photo

ABOUT 90 persons attended the annual meeting of Super 8 Motels Inc., held in Aberdeen at the Holiday Inn. From left are Dennis Bale, president of Super 8 Motels Inc.; Dennis A. Brown, chairman of the board and president of Super 8 Motels West Inc.; Ron Rivett, secretary-treasurer of Super 8 Motels and president of Associated Contractors, and Grant Gard, author, business consultant and professional speaker from Omaha, Neb.

## Super 8 Motel growth noted

DENNIS Bale, president of Super 8 Motel Inc., predicts that by the end of 1977 there will be 45 Super 8 motels operating in the United States.

Bale made his prediction at the Super 8 annual meeting held in Aberdeen. About 90 persons associated with the Super 8 motels in nine states attended the two-day meeting including Dennis Brown, chairman of the board and president of Super 8 Motels West Inc. and Gerald Whitcomb, president of Super

Motels, Washington, Inc. Currently there are 16 Super 8 motels operating in four states with 11 units under construction in five other states.

Super 8 M organized in first motel Aberdeen organiz headquarte deen at 224 Grant usiness

*First Annual*

**SUPER 8 MOTEL**

## CONVENTION

## January 21-22, 1977

ABERDEEN, SOUTH DAKOTA

**T**he program of events at Super 8's first convention included speakers discussing everything from motel liability and accounting procedures to the future of the company. The Aberdeen American News reported that, in his speech, President Dennis Bale predicted there would be 45 motels in the chain by the end of 1977. He was not far off — the actual number at year-end was 35, with another 15 under construction. The convention gave franchisees their first chance to meet one another and learn together, below.

franchise sales when four new license agreements were completed in one morning," a Super 8 newsletter reported. A year later, there were 35 Super 8 motels in seven states, with another 15 under construction.

Already, Super 8 was the fastest-growing economy motel chain in the United States. Room rates, up to $14.88 in 1979, were still a bargain. In 1978, with the opening of motels in Washington and New York States, Super 8 became a coast-to-coast operation. The New York expansion in the town of Montgomery proved especially noteworthy. "I flew out and met George Tolley and Ed Devitt and rolled out my motel prototype on my hotel bed. Up front, I told them they'd be the sole location within two or three states and that there wasn't much we could do to provide them with reservations. But the location they selected was next to a Yellow Freight truck terminal, a destination for scores of drivers, many of whom were also looking for a place to get a good night's sleep in a comfortable

bed. Tolley and Devitt had a home run."

The company pinned high hopes on the newest efforts of Chairman Dennis Brown, who in 1976 moved to California. He had long wanted to live in the Golden State, and planned to develop a group of Super 8 motels there despite its competitive market. Brown opened an office in San Mateo and investigated motel sites throughout the central and northern portions of the state. Due to financing delays, zoning disappointments and red tape, it took three years for Brown's work to bear fruit. In June 1979, construction workers broke ground for the first Super 8 motel in California at an attractive site near the airport in South San Francisco. The 118-room motel opened by the end of the year. Super 8's potential seemed unlimited, and the young chain had already grown far beyond its Midwestern roots.

(Left to right) Loren Steele, Dennis Brown, Dennis Bale, and Ron Rivett formed the original board of directors, a group that carried Super 8 from its infancy to its blossoming into one of America's leading economy chains.

# Not a Fad

**S**uper 8's new corporate headquarters symbolized the company's expansion from an understaffed and space-starved start-up firm to a leader in its industry on a fast track of growth. Five thousand people toured the building during an open house in 1984.

At the end of the 1970s and during the first years of the 1980s, the U.S. economy tossed three obstacles in Super 8's path: high inflation, soaring interest rates and rising gasoline prices. For a young company whose expansion depended so much on predictable construction costs, the availability of loans to franchisees and a steady stream of customers driving along the highways, this economic triple-whammy posed a tremendous threat.

*Many growth milestones quickly flashed by, but Super 8 paused to bottle a special-label Chardonnay to mark its 10th anniversary in 1984.*

As if to confirm the soundness and great potential of the Super 8 business plan, however, the economic challenges of these recessionary years did not slow down the company. "Some lodging companies pulled back, but we accelerated," remembers Harvey Jewett. "We recognized that in recessions, people are trying to save money. Many customers had to move down into our economy category from more expensive motels and hotels. So we kept building."

Dennis Bale, then Super 8's president, remembers the company borrowing money at very high rates of interest — as high as 22 percent. "But when we got through it successfully, we had confidence that there was room in the future for our kind of product," he says.

The numbers justified that kind of confidence. In 1979, Bale told franchisees, "we can boast more construction starts in the last three years than any other budget motel franchise in the nation," and that the gasoline crisis had brought no significant drop in Super 8's occupancy rates. By 1983, Super 8 was opening a new motel nearly once a week — 48 that year alone — bringing the total in the chain to nearly 200. "We didn't pay much attention to the economy," Ron Rivett says. "When we saw gas prices rising, we realized

## Marketing To The Top

Seventh Annual Convention

**Rise Above The Ordinary**

**FEBRUARY 4 & 5, 1983**
**SAN FRANCISCO • AIRPORT HILTON**

*By 1983, the ballooning growth of Super 8 had pushed the company's annual conventions out of Aberdeen and into far-flung cities across the U.S. The San Francisco convention celebrated Super 8's determined efforts to gain a foothold in California.*

business travelers could either do more of their business by phone, which didn't seem likely, or make fewer trips — extending each one for a longer period of time — to cut down on driving. Later we saw companies tell their employees to switch from the Holiday Inns to the economies."

Creative financing fueled expansion. When financing from traditional lenders grew tight, Super 8's management and franchisees explored other avenues. In California, company founder Dennis Brown raised $6.4 million from 1,100 investors in a fully subscribed limited partnership formed to construct new Super 8 motels. He later organized a second California limited partnership to construct even more. Franchisees in Florida, Washington, Texas and other states followed this formula, which allowed for the building of new motels on a cash basis, avoiding the high interest rates of the era.

Several of those limited partnerships have thrived. In 1984, Ron Rivett asked banker Harvey Aman to launch a

**T**he Peninsula Group, headed by Gerry Whitcomb, built Super 8 motels throughout the Pacific Northwest, including this one celebrating its opening in Olympia-Lacey, Washington, in 1980. The national directory from 1980 shows how, with the help of eager franchisees, Super 8 motels were springing up all over the country.

development company to build Super 8 motels in the Mid-Atlantic states. "We raised $4 million, entered into a territorial agreement with Super 8, and received exclusive development rights in Virginia, West Virginia, Maryland, Delaware and the District of Columbia," says Aman, who still heads the partnership. "Over time we have developed 46 Super 8 properties in those states, and in one year, 1986 or 1987, we opened 12."

## Sprouting Along The Highways

Such financing allowed Super 8 to continue recruiting motel developers. "We recruited actively," Jewett says. "Most franchisees were not previously in the motel business. Many were apartment managers, carpenters, plumbers — people from all walks of life. They heard about us through word of mouth, and then we told them about our business support system. We had a construction company, a supply company and management assistance to help them learn about the lodging business. A lot of them went on to be very successful."

Bonnie Golz, today the owner of a motel supply business, basically followed this course to become a Super 8 franchisee. In the late 1970s, Dennis Bale asked Bonnie's

Super 8's corporate reorganization of 1983 transferred the president's title to Loren Steele (right) from Dennis Bale, who then became vice chairman of the board and chief executive officer. At the same time, the company improved its operations by absorbing the affiliate firms that handled motel construction, supplied fixtures and furniture to franchisees, and managed motels for absentee owners.

father-in-law, Cal Golz, to consider a job selling motel franchises to prospective investors. After researching the company and understanding the financial opportunities, Cal himself was sold on the company. "He got my husband, me and other family members together," Bonnie recalls. "He said, 'We're not going to sell motel franchises — we're going to develop motels.'" The family found desirable locations in Great Falls and Billings, Montana, built Super 8 motels there, and eventually owned 10 of them.

Super 8 had already passed several growth milestones almost too quickly to observe them. "I had no clue things would end up as well as they did," says Loren Steele, who became Super 8's president in 1983 after Dennis Bale was appointed chief executive officer. "In the beginning, we thought we might get to 50 motels. The 50th came sooner than we thought. Then when we had a competition to see who would open the 80th motel, we had three properties open on the same day. There was also a major celebration for the 100th property in the early 1980s."

Once Super 8 reached that milestone, the enthusiasm from potential franchisees mounted significantly. Soon the

**D**espite the rising interest rates of the early 1980s, Super 8 threw groundbreaking and ribbon-cutting ceremonies at a dizzying pace. President Dennis Bale (far left) and co-founder Ron Rivett (far right) are among those digging the first spadefuls for the 100th Super 8 property — also in Aberdeen, South Dakota, in 1981. Bale wields the scissors a few months later, at the opening of Aberdeen West.

The Officers and Directors of
Super 8 Motels Inc.
in celebration of the opening of
the one-hundredth Super 8 Motel
cordially extend an invitation for
Cocktails
on Friday, the fourteenth of August
Nineteen hundred and eighty-one
from 6:30 to 8:30 o'clock in the evening
at the Lumber Company
Aberdeen, South Dakota

Regrets only
225-2272

Super 8 further expanded its headquarters in 1986 with the opening of the Rivett Building (below left) adjacent to the new office building it had raised just two years earlier (below right and inset). With its sights set upon becoming the first truly national economy motel chain by the end of the decade, Super 8 needed a larger and more sophisticated corporate office to support the explosion of new locations.

company was opening 80 to 100 properties a year. "This period brought refreshing self-confidence that in all regions of the country we could compete with other economy chains and continue our program," Steele recalls. And no longer could Steele and his wife wine and dine all new Super 8 owners and managers in their Aberdeen home — there wasn't the time or the space!

As new Super 8 locations appeared across the nation, the company's headquarters in South Dakota was experiencing its own growth. The company's longtime home in an Aberdeen office building had 16 employees in a space designed for 4 before an addition was built that somewhat eased the crunch. But the working environment was still much too congested. In 1983 Super 8's corporate office moved into new quarters east of Aberdeen's central district — a 20,000-square-foot building with updated computer facilities and phone systems. In March 1984, 5,000 people toured the premises during a gala open house.

While planning this move, Super 8 management had also taken the opportunity to reorganize the company's

# Too Busy for Crooks

### *How busy can a motel get?*

In 1980, the Super 8 motel in South San Francisco, California, had an experience that demonstrates one can never be too busy. Early that year, two robbers entered the motel, jumped over the front desk and pulled out guns. Before the night manager could respond to the thieves' demand for money, the phone rang. Instinctively, the manager answered the phone, and just at that moment a busload of guests entered the lobby. The gunmen, clearly overwhelmed, fled empty-handed.

structure. In 1983, Super 8 Motels, Inc., merged with its affiliate companies that handled motel construction, supplies and property management. The result was a sleeker Super 8 that could better coordinate the support activities that franchisees so heavily relied upon.

## Computers To the Rescue

Meanwhile, Super 8 struggled to handle a steady surge in calls to its national reservation phone line. When the toll-free reservation line was launched in October 1975, employee JoAnn LaBay took all of the calls, noted the reservation information on a scrap of paper, called the motel to relay the information and discarded the paper. By 1977, the new phone system — called Superline — required two employees, one taking calls from 9 a.m. to 5 p.m. and another from 5 to 10 p.m. As the number of calls increased, a new system was devised with several operators seated around a large turntable with hundreds of little boxes covering its surface — one slot for each motel. Employees took calls, spun the table and placed reservation slips in the proper slots. The top shelf held

**NORTH PLATTE, NEBRASKA**

"Monday morning I received a call from Mrs. Marilyn Wiggers asking me if I lost something valuable in my room during my stay. I told her I lost a diamond out of my ring and she told me the maid had found it in the bathtub and brought it to the front desk. I was elated and overwhelmed at the honesty of the girls involved.

— *Kay S. of Cheyenne, Wyoming*

reservations made for that day, which were immediately phoned to the motels.

As the volume of calls eventually exceeded 1,000 a day from all 50 states, this system grew unwieldy and impractical. So in 1983, the company hired a young computer whiz named Mike Kistner to create a computerized phone reservation system. Kistner first installed new telephone equipment that, for the first time, automatically placed incoming callers on hold when all Superline operators were occupied — no more busy signals. He then set his sights on a more ambitious innovation — a system that would use computers and modems to instantly relay reservation information to the motels.

On April 1, 1984, the new Superline reservation system was ready for action. "We wanted to have special recognition for the first person who called in and made an automated reservation," remembers Kistner, now Super 8's senior vice president of hotel information systems. "We were waiting at 6 a.m. for the first call. Well, the first call was just an information request. But the next call was a reservation, so we grabbed it and made plans to do a big promo with this guest. Later I thought that we'd better verify that the guest showed up at the motel for the reservation. Unfortunately that guest was a no-show, and we hadn't kept information on the second person to call in with a reservation, so we never could do a big promotion."

Despite such problems as the inability of many motel owners to afford new computer equipment and the bugs in the era's modems and phone lines, Superline soon paid off for Super 8 and its franchisees. With operators able to take reservation requests more quickly and accurately, the number of guests using the service soared. By the end of the 1980s, Superline would be receiving 325,000 calls per month.

## The Rise of the V.I.P. Club

Many of those Superline callers were members of the V.I.P. Club, Super 8's preferred customer program. President Dennis Bale had first conceived of the V.I.P. Club back in July 1977. "I was out at another motel in Aberdeen and noticed that they had a program for frequent customers," he says. "I thought it was a good concept, so I went back to the office and said, 'Let's start

NOW IT'S EASY!

We've made it easy

to reserve *America's*

*Finest Economy Lodging*

**SUPER 8 MOTEL** ®

CALL SUPERLINE
**1-800-843-1991**
Toll Free from anywhere
in the United States

h Dakota number no longer necessary)

**S**uper 8 was the first national economy chain to offer guests a centralized, toll-free reservation line. Its origins were modest, featuring a mechanical turntable, below, equipped with reservation slots for each motel. By 1987, however, the Superline reservation department had evolved into a fully staffed and computerized system, above, that could handle 1.3 million calls a year for the chain's 450 properties.

*B*ob Weller uses a "V.I.P. story" to point out how naive CEOs can be sometimes. It seems that back in 1981 or 1982 when he headed up a chain competing with Super 8, some franchise leaders brought to him a little paper card that said, "Super 8 V.I.P. Club." They wanted to begin a frequent traveler program to copy Super 8's idea.

As Weller relates, he told the franchisees with great confidence that they should "... forget such a club. It'll only be a 'flash in the pan.'" Not too smart, according to Weller's own admission, since V.I.P., with more than 6 million members in 1998, accounted for 54 percent of all 800-number reservations.

Apply today

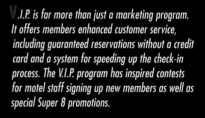

V.I.P. is far more than just a marketing program. It offers members enhanced customer service, including guaranteed reservations without a credit card and a system for speeding up the check-in process. The V.I.P. program has inspired contests for motel staff signing up new members as well as special Super 8 promotions.

one ourselves.'" Super 8 staffers Ron Reed and JoAnn LaBay soon hammered out the details and benefits of membership, and before long, franchisees received application materials to display in the motels. Reed took charge of the program's promotion, LaBay conducted credit checks on applicants, and Cherry Schelle, then Super 8's only secretary, typed and issued V.I.P. Club cards in her spare time.

Driven by benefits that included a 10 percent discount on room rates at participating Super 8 motels, guaranteed reservations without a major credit card and check cashing privileges, guests signed up in large numbers. Membership climbed from 1,000 at the end of 1977 to 5,000 in 1978 and 45,000 in 1982. The first guest to receive an original V.I.P. Club membership card (a paper card typed with membership #001) was vending machine sales representative Nancy Hernandez.

*The original V.I.P. card was hand-typed on a piece of paper. Offering Super 8 guests immediate benefits, such as a 10 percent discount on motel stays, it caught on quickly. Today's V.I.P. card, held by more than 6 million members, represents the most effective marketing promotion in Super 8's history and the preeminent loyalty program in the economy lodging business.*

By 1983, V.I.P. had more than 60,000 members. New magnetic-strip technology would allow motels to quickly swipe and retrieve V.I.P. customer information when guests checked in, but it meant Super 8 had to replace every V.I.P. membership card with a new plastic one. For the next two years, mountains of the old paper cards piled up in Super 8 headquarters until the replacement program was complete.

With the new technology, the V.I.P. Club program marched on to become Super 8's most important marketing program. Its 207,000 members in 1986 included the most loyal Super 8 customers — guests who stayed frequently at Super 8 and felt a fierce attachment to the motels. This army of preferred customers, which would eventually swell to more than 6 million people, formed the core group that would propel Super 8 to the front ranks of economy lodging in the years to come.

# Emerging Giant

J ust 14 years after building its first motel, Super 8 celebrated the opening of its 500th property in College Park, Maryland, in 1988. To millions of travelers in the U.S. and Canada, Super 8 was an essential and welcome roadside presence.

During the 1980s — as hundreds of new Super 8 motels rose along the highways, room reservations poured in by the thousands and armies of guests signed up for the company's preferred customer program — a new breed of businessperson was appearing on the scene in large numbers: Super 8 franchisees and managers. Many who joined this group had never before owned or worked in a motel and needed crucial instruction on the ins and outs of building a successful motel business. Super 8 passed along these crucial lessons as part of the Super 8 training program.

The pineapple has long symbolized hospitality in American and European folklore. Several Super 8 marketing and training programs have borrowed the name and image of the tropical fruit to remind Super 8 staff of their ultimate goal.

The training program traces its roots to the company's earliest years, when new managers and franchisees traveled to the original Aberdeen motel for quarterly training sessions squeezed into a single room — formerly the motel manager's apartment. Back in 1979, when only one of Super 8's motel managers had a college degree in hotel and motel management, the training sessions lasted two weeks and included slide and film presentations on such topics as "Introduction to the Front Desk" and "Courtesy Procedures."

From the earliest effort, Super 8's trainers strove to make motel management understandable to anyone. "We tried to make it basic and simple," says Flo Allen, the company's director of training from 1985 to 1993. "It was simplified training. It included things like how to make a bed and how to clean a bathroom — the basics."

On-site training at motels was first offered in 1983, and the training program in Aberdeen began offering classes year-round two years later.

When Allen first joined the training department, training

**F**lo Allen, director of Super 8 training for several years starting in the mid-1980s, believes that managers and franchisees benefit most from simple training that makes motel management understandable to anyone. Here, in a photo that appeared on the cover of a 1992 issue of Hotel & Resort Industry, Allen coaches motel manager Jerry Glatt.

classes lasted a week, "and it was sometimes a fight to get managers to stay that long," she says. But most managers were eager to learn about marketing, emergency procedures, the use of office and accounting systems and personnel management. Allen remembers one manager in training who "stayed for three weeks and wanted to know how to do everything."

And at least a couple of trainees gained more than an education. In 1986, managers Shirley Freeze and Dick Johnson began a courtship during Super 8 training. They were married two years later.

With the influx of new managers in the late 1980 and 1990s, Super 8's training has grown into a sophisticated program designed to support the company's reputation for cleanliness and friendliness. Trainees using materials from the University of the Pineapple, Super 8's current training program, learn how communication, planning, a clean and friendly product, high standards of performance and dedication are vital elements in the operation of a Super 8 motel.

# THE QUALITY ASSURANCE
# AND TRAINING DEPARTMENT OF
# SUPER 8 MOTELS, INC.

IS PLEASED TO PRESENT THIS CERTIFICATE OF ACHIEVEMENT TO

*Ron Waseka*

UPON COMPLETION OF THE EDUCATIONAL PROGRAM

*Front Desk Sales*

COMPLETED THIS *1st* DAY OF *December*, 19 *84*

*Flo Allen*
DIRECTOR OF QUALITY ASSURANCE & TRAINING

*Charlie Steadmon*
PROGRAM INSTRUCTOR

**B**y the time they complete Super 8's training program, managers, franchisees and staff have gained not only a fine certificate of achievement but also a thorough knowledge of the basics of motel management.

## Of Pineapples and Race Cars

While the company's trainers were educating franchisees and managers, Super 8 also used advertising and promotion to inform the public about the nation's fastest-growing chain of economy motels. At first, the company did little more than its competitors. It issued annual motel directories, promoted its toll-free reservation line, sent mailings to travel agents and provided franchisees with strategies to get free press in their hometown newspapers.

But as Super 8 matured, so did its marketing tactics. In 1981, the company became the first motel chain to advertise on the sides of 18-wheel trucks that each drove about 14,000 highway miles per month. An advertising consultant estimated that these trucks resulted in 101 "visual impressions" per mile. And they targeted Super 8's best customers — business travelers — as they hit the road.

"Eventually the time came when we could do some limited advertising on television and radio," says Loren Steele, who headed the company's marketing efforts for many years. "Our early ads were aimed at the business traveler." During the early 1980s, Super 8 used voluntary contributions from

**S**uper 8's TV commercials have carried viewers everywhere from the football field to the pit of a NASCAR track. The shots above show scenes from a 1990 campaign promoting Superline's toll-free number. The $1 million ad series resulted in 500 million media "impressions." A 1997 TV ad featured NASCAR driver Bill Elliott, right, offering a tour of his Super 8 room — which amusingly housed his tool chest, a rack of racing uniforms and even the tires of his race car.

franchisees to buy air time from such cable networks as CNN and ESPN. One notable commercial, shot in 1983 at the Super 8 motel in Roseville, Minnesota, showed race car driver Bobby Unser checking in at the front desk and watching a replay of his Indy 500 victory on the TV in his room.

Word of mouth and generating repeat business, however, always proved the best kind of marketing. The V.I.P. Club encouraged repeat business better than any-thing else. Other programs designed to introduce Super 8 to new customers also made their mark. During the mid-1980s, countless franchisees used the "We're Pineapple Kind of People" campaign to great effect. Combining sales calls, billboard and radio advertising and old-fashioned enthusiasm, the campaign culminated in handing out some 4,000 pineapples — an ancient symbol of hospitality — to individuals and businesses as a marketing awareness promotion.

## Cleanliness is King

Although gifts of pineapples could demonstrate that Super 8's motels were friendly and welcoming, only frequent inspections would ensure that motels were clean. Super 8 started its inspections program in 1976, when the chain had just 16 motels and 602 rooms. A single employee, Ron Reed, conducted all the quarterly checks.

**A**s Bill Elliott's NASCAR sponsor, Super 8 won the right to display its logo on his uniform and car. This sponsorship and related promotions squarely placed the company before the eyes of millions of guests and potential guests.

*W*hen Christopher Columbus returned to Spain after his visit to the New World in 1492, he brought back pineapples from the West Indian island of Guadeloupe. They became exotic novelties sought after by aristocratic Europeans, who quickly developed a taste for this beautiful, fragrant, rare fruit. A table decorated with pineapples meant that the hosts welcomed their guests to an opulent meal. American colonists also considered the pineapple a sign of welcome. Sea captains would bring pineapples home and set them on their gatepost as a signal to friends that they were welcome to visit. Carvings of the fruit frequently adorned entryways and guest beds. Today the pineapple remains a symbol of hospitality and friendliness.

Doug Vogt, today the director of quality assurance, joined Super 8 in 1984 as an inspector. Then one of just four inspectors, he conducted about 400 Super 8 inspections a year in all corners of the U.S. "I remember that the first one I did on my own was in Riverton, Wyoming. I was scared to death," he says. "Fortunately that property scored 'Excellent,' the best grade we gave at the time." Back then, the checks were scheduled in advance, but since the late 1980s inspectors have arrived unannounced.

Hitting the road for three weeks at a time, Vogt visited about 85 percent of all the Super 8 properties during the mid- to late-1980s. Young and unattached, he enjoyed life on the road, and the relationship between inspectors and franchisees was always good. "The best part was seeing the chain grow from about 200 properties to where it is now," he says. On one notable trip he inspected a motel room with a bad odor that confounded housekeepers. Wedged in the boxspring he discovered a dead rabbit. In a chain that places such a high value on cleanliness, such occurrences are rare.

Since the early 1990s, about 95 percent of Super 8 properties have passed their inspections. With the goal of providing a clean and safe environment, Super 8 is the only major economy chain that inspects its motels four times each year and that requires motels to use detectors designed to warn against unsafe levels of propane and other natural gasses.

"Overall, the quality has remained very constant because we have so many long-term Super 8 owners," Vogt says. "Quality assurance inspects the properties, but the credit for our cleanliness goes to the owners — the ones who pay the bills and make a commitment to clean motels."

Maid Duties

## Room Cleaning Procedures

1. If rooms are not in the condition indicated on the housekeeper's slip, report this immediately to the housekeeper.

2. Always keep the cart close to the wall s... by easily. Be sure to smile when guest p... or such greeting as is proper, but do n...

3. OPEN WINDOWS AND DOOR TO AIR OUT THE RO... Nothing else keeps rooms and halls smel...

4. Turn on air-conditioner and heating uni... working properly.

5. Turn on the television set to make sure... in good working condition. Adjust col... necessary. Report defects to housekee...

6. Empty all partly filled glasses in toi...

7. Empty ashtrays and waste baskets in tr... are no hot ashes in contents.

8. Remove bedspread and fold carefully.

9. Remove pillow cases.

10. Place pillows on the chair.

11. Remove blankets and place on top of p...

12. Remove sheets. Shake pillow cases, b... removing them to expose any valuables...

13. Check all linen, spreads and blankets... Report any damage to the housekeeper...

14. Strip bathroom of soiled linen.

15. Put a small amount of detergent in t...

16. Wash bath...

17. Rinse an... stay on... water sp...

18. Wash and...

19. Clean sh...

20. Wash toi... seat.

21. Scrub toi...

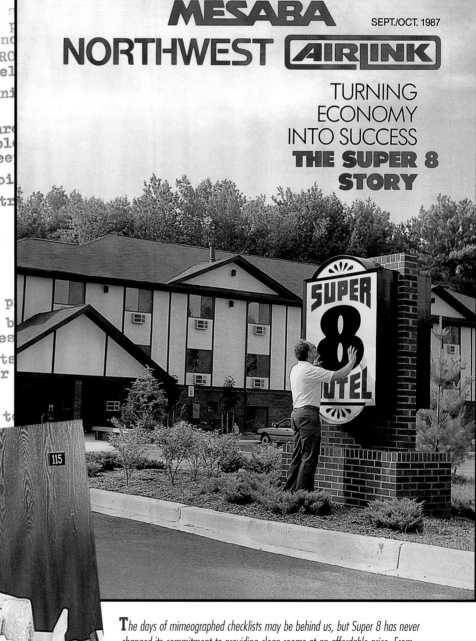

**T**he days of mimeographed checklists may be behind us, but Super 8 has never changed its commitment to providing clean rooms at an affordable price. From the earliest days, each motel was expected to meet strict standards for cleanliness. A 1987 magazine article in Mesaba, a Northwest Airlink publication, cited the company's quality assurance program as one of the factors behind Super 8's rapid growth and continuing appeal to business travelers.

**C**o-founder Dennis Brown, inset, died in 1988, leaving behind a company that that was strong, growing and ready to lead its industry. After his death, Super 8 commissioned for its headquarters a bronze sculpture depicting Brown's dedication to his family. Barbara Brown and her three daughters gathered around the sculpture Family after its unveiling.

## The Passing of a Founder

In December 1985, Super 8 Founder and Chairman Dennis Brown felt a soreness in his stomach — the first symptom of a disease that ended his life 26 months later at the age of 47 in San Mateo, California. Although his leiomyosarcoma (cancer of the smooth muscle tissue) and his medical treatment steadily sapped his energy, he remained an inspiration to the Super 8 family during the months of his illness and after his death.

Flo Allen, former director of training, last saw Brown in 1986 when he addressed Super 8 franchisees at the company's annual convention in Phoenix. "I'll never forget that day. He was in a full-body cast but had on a pinstripe suit and a tie," she recalls. "His talk was so inspiring. The people who never met that man missed out on a rare opportunity. He never forgot a name, and was a tremendous, soft and gentle person."

"Although by the time of his illness he was not much involved in the daily operations of Super 8," says then-CEO Dennis Bale, "his commitment to the company was extraordinary. "He would come back to Aberdeen once a year, walk through the headquarters and pump everyone up. The staff would tell each other, 'Dennis is here!' He'd tell you something — just making conversation — but later you'd realize there was an important message in what he said. He examined everything in the industry to see how it could apply to Super 8 and was always years ahead of the rest of us."

After Brown's death, Super 8 established the Dennis Brown Memorial Award, which goes to franchisees who have developed eight or more properties. The name of Dennis Brown continues to live on in the work of some of the organization's most successful and dynamic motel owners.

## Making Super 8 Grow

Quality assurance, marketing and well-trained personnel brought guests back to Super 8 motels, but franchisees — who develop new motels and invest in improvements to current properties — kept Super 8 growing. The 1980s and early 1990s marked an unprecedented growth in the number of Super 8 motels. Between 1985 and 1992, the chain's properties soared in number nearly 200 percent — from 323 to 942 in 48 states plus Canada — and the total number of Super 8 rooms climbed from 20,247 to 57,633.

Dale Aasen, now a regional vice president of franchise sales, joined Super 8 in 1985 with the assignment of developing franchisees in several states. "Seventy percent of our franchise sales from 1985 to 1993 went to existing franchisees," he notes. "At

*The sculpture of Brown and his daughters inspired the design of the Dennis Brown Memorial Award. The award is given annually to franchisees who break into the ranks of those owning eight or more Super 8 motels.*

# Champion Bedmakers

*I*n 1991, at Super 8's International Convention in Orlando, Florida, a group of skilled employees from Super 8 properties took the center stage to demonstrate their craft and compete against one another. They had no specialized tools — just their arms, brains and quick feet. For the first time, Super 8 was about to crown its champion bedmaker, and the winner would receive a new car.

The winner of that first International Bedmaking Championship was Deb Schneider, head housekeeper of the Super 8 motel in (East) Aberdeen, South Dakota. Since then, the crown has passed to six other housekeepers, who show their speed in making a bed while adhering to Super 8's rigorous quality standards.

Those standards require bedmakers to lay sheets tightly, without wrinkles and with all corners mitered; to set blankets straight, four to six inches from the headboard and with the "Super 8 Tuck" that folds the top sheet four to six inches over the blanket; to stuff pillows into pillowcases without holding the pillow under the chin (not the most sanitary way to do it); to set pillows straight, the open end of the pillowcase facing the edge of the bed; and to lay bedspreads without wrinkles and with mitered corners at the foot. Breaking the standards in this contest produces penalties, and with four penalties bedmakers are out.

"I do not practice for the contest," says Delaine Klabo, an Aberdeen (West) housekeeper who consistently makes beds in two and a half minutes, won the championship in 1997, and advanced to the finals in 1999. "I've been with Super 8 for 10 years and make the beds the same way in the competition as I do in the motel."

The international championship event, now held before the public at the Mall of America in Bloomington, Minnesota, is raucous and crowded with spectators. The competitors have each passed a regional championship in order to appear in the finals. Music blasts from large speakers as the bedmakers work. The crowd cheers the contestants, boos the judges and waves Super 8 "clackers," producing an echoing noise. When a judge pronounces, "This bed is OK," the roar is deafening.

And the beds are more than OK. They are perfect.

*Deb Schneider of Aberdeen, South Dakota, top, posed with her new Geo Metro after winning the first Super 8 Bedmaking Championship in 1991. The competition tests the speed, attention to detail, and dedication to perfection of housekeepers like Cindy Benton, below, of the Fairmont, Minnesota, Super 8 motel, who competed in the 1999 championship at the Mall of America in Minneapolis, Minnesota. At recent championships, the percussive sound of Super 8 clappers, left, has heightened the excitement as the housekeepers compete.*

*Super 8's company officers gathered in 1989 for a rare group photo. They had much to celebrate that year, with 41,000 motel rooms in service nationwide and Superline handling as many as 325,000 reservation calls a month. During the next few years, they would guide Super 8 into one of the most exciting periods of its history.*

first we had no TV ads or brochures to attract people — it was all word of mouth. Then we began advertising in lodging trade publications and at trade shows." All prospective franchisees, he says, paid their own way to Aberdeen to see Super 8's reservation system and headquarters. "When they saw all that support, it was an easy sale. We treated franchisees as family," he adds.

Aasen remembers one prospective franchisee in Ohio who couldn't decide whether to invest in a motel. "I told him, 'Don't wait — it's now or never.' So he bought a franchise. I met him later, and he said, 'I only wish you got me in earlier,'" Aasen says.

Super 8 co-founder Ron Rivett still recalls the thrill he felt in 1975 when a motel developer in Gillette, Wyoming, handed him a check for $10,000 and became the first Super 8 franchisee. "At that time we didn't have much to offer him other than operating support," Rivett says. "We couldn't give him reservations, but we could give plans, tell him how to put the financing together and get through the building process and show him how to operate the motel." As the years passed, Super 8 continued to give franchisees that kind of support, along

with much more: reservations, a position of leadership in the lodging industry and, most importantly, consistency and high standards that guests learned to seek out and expect. This was the solid base that prepared Super 8 and its franchisees for the challenges and successes that the 1990s would bring.

## MOTEL TALES

Several years ago, I accepted a position with a company that required me to travel extensively. I started out in my truck assuming that I would sample several hotel chains and find three or four that I really liked. However, it didn't take me long to discover that the best hotel chain in the country is Super 8. I have always encountered professionalism, courtesy, friendliness and helpfulness at so many of your sites. I would just like to say, "Thanks for having truck parking, outside outlets, continental breakfast, cable TV, recliners, free local calls and a friendly, helpful and professional Superline staff."

*Kevin H., Denver, Colorado*

# The Leader

**W**hen Super 8 reached the magical number of 888 franchised properties in 1992 with the opening of this motel in Thurmont, Maryland, the company seemed at the height of its powers. Few could have predicted that the company would more than double its size in the next seven years during a period of dynamic growth in the 1990s.

**B**y the early 1990s, Super 8 had attained unprecedented size — nearly 1,000 motels — and a position of leadership in the economy motel industry, all under the direction of the same group of people who had founded and launched the company two decades before. Ron Rivett, an original owner of Super 8 and builder of the very first motel in the chain, was beginning to believe that it might be time for a change. He discussed his feelings with Loren Steele, Harvey Jewett and other company officers.

In 1993, Super 8 went from homegrown ownership into the fold of Hospitality Franchise Systems, Inc. Though some feared the influence of an East Coast company, HFS — which merged to become Cendant in 1997 — respected the winning formula Super 8 had developed and supported even more rapid growth during the 1990s.

"I told them that the company was super big and was going strong and doing well. But I was worried that we were burning out — running out of gas. I had always considered stress to be my fuel, and I couldn't get too much of it. But after Dennis Brown's death, my attitude changed. The company seemed so big, and I wasn't doing so much of the fun stuff anymore. I said, 'Let's explore the possibility of selling.'"

Loren Steele, then vice chairman of the board, agreed. "We felt we had taken the company as far as we could as entrepreneur-managers, and now it was time for professional managers to slip into place."

Super 8 entertained several potential buyers, but the strongest suitor was New Jersey-based Hospitality Franchise Systems, Inc., (HFS), a company that in its short three-year history had already grown into a lodging-industry giant, acquiring the franchising rights to the Ramada, Howard Johnson and Days Inn hotel chains. Eventually, in addition to Super 8,

HFS would also own the Travelodge, Villager Lodge, Wingate Inn and Knights Inn chains, as well as several of the nation's largest real estate brokerage firms.

Super 8 joined the HFS family in April 1993. "For all of us it was an emotional day," remembers Loren Steele. "There were tears in my eyes. But the decision was right."

At this important moment in Super 8's history, Ron Rivett thought of his longtime partner, Dennis Brown. "One feeling I had at the closing of the sale was missing Dennis," Rivett says. "He would have enjoyed that day, seeing the full success we had."

Franchisees regarded the sale cautiously, unsure of what was to follow. Many shared values of trust and friendliness that they feared a new parent might not embrace. "There was concern that a company from back East might not run the company the same way we did," says Bill Bowen, a Super 8 corporate attorney at the time of the sale. "There's always fear of the unknown."

The heroes given this award, which goes monthly to employees nominated by their coworkers at Super 8's Aberdeen Reservation Center, have been recognized for the high quality of their work. Winners receive an acrylic star and a cash award. Super 8 has long emphasized recognizing employees for outstanding service and on-the-job achievement.

**T**his 1997 cookbook proved that Super 8 staff could whip up a meal with the same expertise they do their jobs — that HFS ownership did not mean the end of Super 8 culture. The cookbook included the names of all employees who created the hundreds of recipes in the book. With its deep experience as a lodging franchisor, Cendant offers Super 8 franchisees a wealth of resources to draw upon in developing their properties. These include architectural plans for different motel prototypes, right, referrals to experienced motel builders and financial guidance.

**E**ach Super 8 convention produces its own assortment of mementos. Event tickets, name badges, private-label salsa and a bandana sum up the atmosphere and excitement of the 1995 convention, held in Dallas.

RESERVED SEATING

SATURDAY, MARCH 11

Awards Banquet

INTERNATIONAL CONVENTION
"Texas Style"
It's gonna be HOT

1974 SUPER 8 MOTEL 1994

Celebrating Our 20th Anniversary

**Barbara**
Barbara Michlitsch
Super 8 Motels, Inc.
Aberdeen SD

DENNIS BROWN MEMORIAL DINNER

May 7, 1990

Brocket Hall
London, England

6:30 P.M. Cocktails
7:30 P.M. Dinner

The Board of Directors
of
Super 8 Enterprises, Inc.
requests your presence
at the Dennis Brown Memorial Dinner
being held in your honor
on this date.

RSVP to:
Bridget Engler
Super 8 Motels, Inc.
1910 N. E. Eighth Avenue
Aberdeen, SD 57401

**G**atherings, formal and informal, have remained an important part of the company's culture, especially as its rapid growth spreads the Super 8 name farther afield. This retreat to the Campbell River in British Columbia in 1988, above and inset, was an important opportunity for Super 8 executives to relax and strategize. Another important tradition was the owners conference, which evolved to include the Dennis Brown Memorial Dinner and prestigious locations, such as Brocket Hall in London, left, where the Memorial Dinner was held in 1990.

During the 1990s, Super 8 experienced rapid growth. Some representative properties of the decade include the motel in Prince Frederick, Maryland, top, which opened in 1998, a 1996 property in Ferndale, Washington, bottom, and a Super 8 motel that opened in Redmond, Oregon, center, in 1997. The Peninsula Group developed the latter two properties.

Number of motels in Canada – approaching *75*

Number of rooms per motel (average) – *61*

Number of V.I.P. Club members – over *6 million*

Number of rooms – approaching *115,000*

Number of motels – approaching *1,900*

As quickly became apparent, however, the new ownership gave Super 8 many advantages. As a franchisor of several other lodging brands, HFS could apply its franchising and marketing expertise to Super 8. And with its greater financial resources, HFS could invest extensively in such important areas as technology, training and quality assurance.

HFS further reassured franchisees with its appointment of Bob Weller as the new president of Super 8. "Weller was a genius choice," says Paul Schulte, an early Super 8 franchisee and now a partner in Supertel, one of Super 8's largest property owners. "He quickly won the respect, admiration and trust of franchisees."

Weller, a former motel owner and a 20-year veteran of the economy lodging industry, had first encountered Super 8 in the mid-1970s as the head of the competing Econo Lodges of America chain. "It was the most friendly competitive relationship I had with any chain in the country," he says. "The Super 8 people were always a group of gentlemen. In their quiet way they blew right past us, and when other chains were out tooting their horns, Super 8 was settling into business."

When he took the helm of Super 8, Weller recalls, he knew that it was not a company that needed fixing. "It was a very good company already on a strong growth trend. It was the challenge of my career to keep Super 8 on track, build on its success, and make it even better if I could. I wanted to remain focused on the same basics of hospitality — clean rooms and friendly service — that have run consistently through Super 8's history," he says.

Tom McNulty, whom Weller hired as Super 8's vice

A COASTAL COMMUNICATIONS CORPORATION PUBLICATION        AUGUST 1994  VOL.17  NO.8

THE MAGAZINE FOR LODGING MANAGEMENT

# HOTEL & RESORT

## INDUSTRY

HOSPITALITY FRANCHISE S

Cover Story Page 18
BOB WELLER & CO.
**Super 8's Super Team**

ALSO IN THIS ISSUE: ■ THE BOOMER BOOM
■ SATISFYING GUESTS BY THE BOOK ■ PRODUCT REVIEW: OPL EQUIPMENT
■ BENCHMARKING: SIGNPOSTS FOR SURVIVAL

*In 1994, a year after Super 8 became an HFS company, Hotel & Resort Industry magazine profiled the new management team of President and Chief Operating Officer Bob Weller and Super 8's franchisee advisory board, above. "When you add the umbrella services of an HFS to a highly successful company like Super 8," Weller told the magazine, "it's like a guy walking into a bar with a 2,000-pound gorilla for a bodyguard."*

president of marketing in 1994, echoes those sentiments. "When I arrived, the plan I followed was 'Don't screw up a good thing,'" he says. "The previous owners had done such a good job of building the culture of the company and its reputation for friendliness and cleanliness. I didn't want to ruin this gift or try to make Super 8 into something else. Super 8 understands who it is."

## North American Expansion

Under the new management of HFS, which merged to become Cendant in 1997, Super 8's growth accelerated, expanding the chain to nearly 1,900 motels by the end

*In May 1999 Super 8 opened its 1,800th motel, a property in Calgary-Shawnessy, Alberta. In addition to further spotlighting Super 8's continuing growth and reinforcing Cendant's position as the leading lodging franchisor, this milestone symbolized the importance to Super 8 of the rapidly expanding Canadian market.*

of the century. One of the areas of fastest growth was Canada, which Super 8 had entered in 1981. Marc Staniloff, president of Royop Properties Corporation, was operating an unbranded family-owned motel in Calgary in 1992 when a franchising agent told him about Super 8. "I had traveled in the States but had never stayed in a Super 8 motel or even heard of it," he says. "I checked it out."

Staniloff liked what he learned. At a time when there were only six existing Super 8 properties in Canada, he purchased the right to develop motels in western Canada and eventually throughout the entire country. He converted his family motel to a Super 8 motel in July 1994, and "it was like the floodgates opened up," he says. "Our gross sales went up 40 percent instantly. That really caught our attention." Staniloff also noticed that about 35,000 V.I.P. Club members lived in Alberta, with another one million in the bordering provinces and states. "That was a sign of very strong brand recognition," he observes.

Royop now projects that it will own 100 Super 8 properties in 2000. "We've had Super 8 people from the States who look at our market and say, 'That's exactly where we were 15 years ago.' Look at a map and you can see we have huge opportunities," Staniloff says.

Sharing in this growth have been the U.S. franchisees, some of whom have developed up to 50 Super 8 properties. These franchisees include Super 8 Motel Development, with 39 motels in the Mid-Atlantic states; the Rivett Group, holders of 40 motels formerly under Super 8's corporate ownership; and Supertel, with 58 motels, primarily in the Midwest.

But owners of smaller numbers of properties still remain important in Super 8's growth formula. One such owner is Dick Barry, whose three motels in Wisconsin have consistently won quality assurance awards. A former supper club owner, Barry built his first Super 8 motel in 1984. "I wanted a franchise that

*Every time a guest writes in with compliments on the service they have received at a Super 8 motel, the responsible employee wins a Super Star ribbon. After earning eight such ribbons, the employee gets an 8 Star Service Award. These recognitions show guests that Super 8 listens to customer comments and rewards employees for delivering exceptional service.*

## MOTEL TALES

### SPOKANE, WASHINGTON

While we frequent your Super 8 motel, we had no idea that it would become our home away from home. When my husband had a heart attack in the motel, he was forced to undergo open-heart surgery. The motel staff sent beautiful flowers, and every night when I came in from a day at the hospital, someone was there to offer help and support. On the day my husband was released, the staff threw him a welcome home party at the motel. We will never forget their endless support.

*Bud & Lisa B., Den Bosch, Netherlands*

*A*s of August 1999, 1,751 Super 8 motels offered guests the chance to make on-line reservations. These are the motels that boasted the largest number of bookings made on the Web:

**Washington, D.C.**

**Las Vegas (Koval Lane), Nevada**

**Anaheim (Katella Avenue), California**

**Hayward (I-880), California**

**Seattle, Washington**

**Moab, Utah**

**Elk Grove, Illinois**

**New Orleans, Louisiana**

**San Diego (Sea World), California**

**San Antonio (I-35) airport, Texas**

was development oriented with a concept that was still fairly new to the Midwest," he says. "I learned to run the motel through Super 8's corporate training."

"We've always taken pride in bringing in people with no lodging experience," says Dale Aasen, "There is such a wide and deep talent pool to help them. We've had so many success stories, and many started out as Mom and Pop owners."

The word is spreading. In late 1998, *Success* magazine rated Super 8 the best franchising opportunity in the lodging industry, and *Entrepreneur* followed by ranking Super 8 as the fastest growing motel chain.

The growth of Super 8 during the 1990s has come despite a devaluation of real estate in the early years of the decade and a later influx of economy motel competitors. "In the last five to six years there has been explosive growth in the nation's lodging inventory," explains Harvey Jewett, now president and COO of the Rivett Group. Many new motels fall into the economy category but still include such amenities as swimming pools, spas, exercise areas, business centers, continental breakfasts and meeting rooms. Super 8 has kept pace — and at the same time, it has kept a consistent image for guests. "They call us the McDonald's of motels," marketing vice president Tom McNulty notes. "That's a compliment. Guests tell us they know what to expect from a Super 8 motel."

In the days since Dennis Brown and Ron Rivett opened their very first motel in Aberdeen, South Dakota, almost every aspect of the business has grown and changed beyond everyone's wildest imagination. Everything except the philosophy — clean and friendly. That's what guests have expected for the past 25 years, and thanks to the franchisees and employees who serve them, that's what Super 8 Motels will continue to be.

**S**uper 8 has been celebrating its 25th anniversary throughout 1999 by issuing such collectibles as birthday announcements, commemorative shirts, and balloons bearing the anniversary logo. The culmination of this milestone year is a grand birthday celebration in October.

# Timeline

**1972**
Dennis Brown tries to organize a loose association of budget Midwestern motels under the Super 8 name. The effort eventually fails.

**1973**
Dennis Brown and Ron Rivett meet in an Aberdeen, South Dakota, coffee shop and discuss launching a chain of budget motels.

**1974**
Brown and Rivett build and open the first Super 8 Motel, in Aberdeen. The room rate is $8.88.

Super 8 hires its first employee, Ron Reed.

**1975**
The first franchised Super 8 Motel opens, in Gillette, Wyoming.

Super 8 opens Superline, its national toll-free reservation line.

**1976**
The inspections program begins, judging the quality of the 602 rooms in all 16 Super 8 properties.

Dennis Bale becomes the company's new president.

The number of franchised motels reaches 22.

**1977**
The company holds its first convention for franchisees, in Aberdeen.

The V.I.P. Club officially opens. It soon grows into the biggest and best loyalty program in the budget motel business.

**1978**
The opening of motels in the states of Washington and New York makes Super 8 a coast-to-coast operation.

**1979**
Super 8 opens its first California motel, fulfilling co-founder Dennis Brown's dream.

**1981**
Super 8 franchises its first Canadian motel, in North Battleford, Saskatchewan.

The 100th Super 8 Motel opens its doors, in (West) Aberdeen, South Dakota.

**1982**
V.I.P. Club membership stands at 45,000.

**1983**
The company opens a record 48 motels in a single year, bringing the total number to nearly 200.

Loren Steele succeeds Dennis Bale as Super 8 president; Bale becomes chief executive officer.

The company's affiliated businesses handling motel construction, supplies and property management merge with Super 8 into a streamlined organization.

The training department introduces on-site training at motels.

Super 8 moves its corporate headquarters to its own new building in Aberdeen.

**1984**
Superline undergoes a conversion to fully computerized operations.

**1986**
V.I.P. membership climbs to 207,000.

**1986**
Super 8 adds a second headquarters building, the Rivett Building.

**1988**
The 500th Super 8 property opens in College Park, Maryland.

Dennis Brown, who founded Super 8 with Ron Rivett, dies from cancer.

**1991**
Deb Schneider, head housekeeper at the Super 8 in (East) Aberdeen, South Dakota, wins the first Super 8 International Bedmaking Championship.

**1992**
Super 8 opens its 888th motel, in Thurmont, Maryland.

**1993**
Hospitality Franchise Systems, Inc., purchases Super 8 and makes it a part of its well-established family of lodging brands, such as Ramada Inn, Howard Johnson and Days Inn.

Bob Weller joins Super 8 as president and chief operating officer.

**1997**
Hospitality Franchise Systems changes its name to Cendant.

**1998**
V.I.P. hits 6 million members, who account for 54 percent of the company's 800-number reservations.

*Success* rates Super 8 the best franchising opportunity in the lodging industry, and *Entrepreneur* ranks it as the fastest-growing motel chain.

**1999**
As its 25th anniversary nears, Super 8 anticipates celebrating several milestones: 1,900 motels, 100 Canadian motels and 115,000 guest rooms.

please do not disturb

SUPER 8 MOTEL

## Acknowledgments

Many people share the credit for helping nurture this book from its beginnings as a spark of an idea to its completion.

My biggest thanks go to Barb introduced me to the company, with pride, and connected me and Jan Waltman tirelessly dug up boxes of stuff to me, answered important interviews. Many Michlitsch of Super 8, who showed me its facilities and staff with many helpful people. Barb research materials, shipped heavy my questions and scheduled all- thanks to Bob Weller and Tom McNulty, who saw the value in this project and supported the efforts of everyone involved. • I also want to thank everyone who generously set aside time to let me interview them and tap their memory. In particular, I thank Ron Rivett, Barbara Brown, Bob Weller, Tom McNulty, Harvey Jewett, Loren Steele, Dennis Bale, Harvey Aman, Marc Staniloff, Dale Aasen, Flo Allen, Dick Barry, Bill Bowen, Pat Fussell, Bonnie Golz, Milo Graff, Mike Kistner, Delaine Klabo, Irene Roberts, Paul Schulte and Doug Vogt. To all the Super 8 staff and franchisees who have contributed to the wonderful 25-year saga of this company, I tip my hat. Your achievements made my work a pleasure. — *Jack El-Hai, September 1999*